EYES OPEN

LONDON

IDEO EYES OPEN

LON
DON

Fred Dust + IDEO

A field guide for the curious

CHRONICLE BOOKS
SAN FRANCISCO

Library of Congress Cataloging-in-Publication Data available.

ISBN: 978-0-8118-6173-1

Manufactured in China.

Designed by Sara Frisk.
Written by Amy Leventhal.

10 9 8 7 6 5 4 3 2 1

Chronicle Books LLC
680 Second Street
San Francisco, California 94107
www.chroniclebooks.com

AT IDEO, IDENTIFYING INTERESTING THINGS, EXPLORING NEW EXPERIENCES, AND INSPIRING OTHERS IS A LARGE PART OF OUR JOB.

Sometimes it's about finding truly unique experiences in the world—you'll find several described in this book. But more often, we focus on normal, everyday things and seeing what's interesting about them.

There are a lot of different methods we use to look at the world. If you've seen *IDEO Method Cards*, you've already seen a few. But often, when trying to tease out what's unique or intriguing about an experience, there are really just two things we try to keep in mind: go broad and dig deep.

GOING BROAD: Widening your perspective to include multiple experiences allows you to make some interesting connections. Mapping your observations helps reveal larger patterns of behavior that can explain why an experience is meaningful or why it might miss the mark. When enough similarities present themselves across experiences, even broader patterns of cultural norms emerge.

We use cross-references to prompt connections that tie one entry to another. At certain points throughout the book, we pull ideas out to create moments of pause. These theme pages reflect some of the many patterns that emerge through observation, immersion, and experience. They represent an elaboration on the larger themes that emerge as you move through the city. Additionally, while the main image on each entry spread always relates to the featured location, the space above it occasionally references a destination that does not appear elsewhere in the book. When you see an [✳] icon, we hope you will be intrigued enough to seek out these locations on your own.

DIGGING DEEP: We look at things all the time, but less often do we ponder and see what's actually happening. Next time you're out and about, try to think about the myriad behaviors you observe and what might inspire them. For example, do they emerge from within an individual, or are they prompted by something external? Really watching people and what they're doing will help you identify and learn from these things as they happen.

Likewise, asking is often a great way to gain more clarity about why things happen the way they do. A little bit of conversation can lead to a wealth of inspiration. In this book, we try to include backstory that we find revealing. In some cases, there are even pictures of the people who crafted the experiences, because so much of who they are and what they believe is evident in the expression of their ideas.

Looking through one lens provides only one perspective. At IDEO, we bring multiple views and complementary strengths to bear on all our projects. This approach allows us to inspire each other and constructively challenge and build upon one another's ideas, resulting in unified, coherent solutions to complex design problems. We chose to tackle this book in the same way, pulling together a diverse team of designers. To learn a bit more about our process and our team, check out the "How This Book Happened" section in back.

As you go through the book, you'll likely find places you won't want to visit, as well as places that you may already have been. Regardless, we hope you find something unique in every entry. Each was chosen to help open your eyes to a new way of perceiving. Sometimes it's about recognizing a pattern of behavior or uncovering a latent need. Sometimes it's about teasing out design ingenuity, and, every once in a while, we simply heard a good story that we wanted to share.

Each time you visit a city, you experience a snapshot in time. The next time you go, the city reveals another side of itself. That said, don't use this book to plan your trip, and don't be sad if what you are looking for is no longer there. That's what's most exciting about exploring: Nothing is ever the same thing twice. Including your own perspective.

But hopefully, if we got *Eyes Open* right, it might inspire you to see something a little bit differently, whether you're in a foreign city or your own backyard.

Fred

LONDON

SURRENDER YOURSELF AND ADMIT THAT YOU LOVE IT.

Whether you live here or are just visiting, London holds a lot of mystique: charming, densely populated, maybe smaller in some places and roomier in others, and there are some places that are just plain impossible to understand. But, on the whole, it's as familiar as a fairy tale, and if you just admit that you love it straightaway, you can dispense with feeling like a stranger.

THINGS AREN'T ALWAYS AS YOU'D SUSPECT.

There's a funny kind of pattern to London that alternates between exhausting intensity and utter calm. You can experience it by simply turning the corner from a bustling high street onto a calm lane or stepping out from the frenzy of the Tube into a peaceful neighborhood. It's not just about where you are—it's about when you are somewhere. The jam-packed craze of a Sunday morning market can disappear in an hour's time. The sprawling, frantic drunkenness of a Friday night can collapse into the desolation of a trash-filled street on a Saturday morning.

YOU CAN'T REALLY CAPTURE LONDON IN A SOUND BITE—OR FIFTY.

The fact is we tried. The entries in this book are meant to reflect unique experiences in themselves, while also working together as a whole to reveal the overall character of the city. The themes, found on the pictureless pages, suggest broad patterns that helped us understand London—the place and the people within—a little better. Some pages describe how the city is inhabited (see "Rooftops" or "Traces of the Past"). Some are about membership and interaction (see "A Sense of Belonging" or "Communal Tables"). And some are simply examples of things Londoners do better than anyone else (see "More" or "Bathrooms of London").

Wherever we go, themes remind us that "they do things differently here." When you look at the themes in the *Eyes Open* series in one go, you'll see a broader picture, revealing the quirkiness and complexities that make London a city you can't help but adore.

TRADE IN EXPECTATIONS
FOR EXPLORATIONS.

Within a day, those just visiting London will be speaking with a different cadence. Even the e-mails we sent started including words like "cheeky" and "rather." You'll meet people in your travels who are from somewhere else but have lived in London for years, and you'll notice the ways in which they've adapted their speech and mannerisms. You'll grow comfortable with wandering. The city puts you under a spell that makes exploring a necessity. Afternoons disappear into evenings, making it hard to recall all you have been up to and where you have been.

When exploring new places, it's natural to try and control the experience with maps, schedules, plans. But as we learned in creating this book, sometimes it's better to let a city like London just happen to you. There may be mornings that you miss breakfast because you lost track of time at a members-only bar the night before. Sometimes getting slightly lost will mean that a market will be closed down by the time you get there. You'll want to do it all, but of course, you never can. So cut yourself some slack, catch what you can, stay from your itinerary and your expectations, and fall in love with London.

GETTING AROUND

TO HELP GET YOU STARTED, HERE ARE A FEW MODES THAT WE FOUND CONVENIENT, HELPFUL, AND EASY TO USE AS VISITORS IN A CITY THAT IS NOT OUR OWN.

A city as diverse and spread out as London offers multiple ways of getting where you need to go. How you choose to navigate will directly affect the way you see and understand the city. Great cities have great transportation systems that are iconic of the cities themselves. Each system enables you to see that city in a very specific way. Be open to trying different modes at different times. Take mood and weather into consideration. See what opportunities each presents. And remember, getting there can be an interesting adventure and learning experience in and of itself—great for people-watching, chatting with locals, getting your bearings, or just taking a breather.

BY FOOT

If you've got the luxury of time, the best way to get around and really take in what the city has to offer is by foot. It allows you to enjoy some of the city's subtle nuances you otherwise might miss. It helps you understand how one neighborhood connects to another. And it allows you to set your own pace. Pace, of course, is everything. It's the difference between wearing yourself out and hitting your stride. This can be challenging when traveling with others who may define those things differently than you do. Check in with each other from time to time and make sure it's working for everyone.

This should be fairly obvious, but wear comfortable shoes. They can greatly affect your outlook on the day, for better or worse. No matter what you wear, if you're exploring for long stretches of time, at some point your feet are going to hurt, and that's when you might consider other modes of getting around.

BY BLACK CAB

From its iconic, polished exterior to its generous interior with fold-down seats and plenty of room for people or packages, the black cab is often said to be the greatest purpose-built vehicle. The black cab is the cabbie's space, not yours. You ask to come in, you pay when you get out, and in the interim it is the cabbie's whim as to whether or not he or she will entertain you with a theatrical monologue through the backseat speakers.

In the dense parts of the city, the cab is actually a good equivalent to walking. You can stop as needed and there's always another one nearby. At night or in distant neighborhoods, the assuredness of the cabbies driving on roads unfamiliar to you can be thrilling and almost Disneyesque.

BY TUBE

From the outside looking in, it seems that Londoners think of their world in terms of Tube stops. Even when using other modes of transportation, Tube stops become neighborhood landmarks. Some stations are above ground and offer fresh air and natural light. Some have escalators so long they seem to take you deep within the core of the Earth. Emerge from one station and you might find yourself in a place that feels identical to where you started. Or, you may emerge in places that don't feel like London at all.

ONE WORD OF ADVICE:

Have a sense of where you are going and what you are doing before heading for the turnstiles, especially at rush hours. Everyone seems short on time and low on patience. While down in the tunnels leading to and from the trains, you're going to want to swim with the current to avoid feeling like a foreigner. Once underground, the Tube is its own world with subterranean services and its own kind of currency. The system seems to have its own weather (slightly damp), its own language (the iconic and colorful Tube map), and its own set of rules.

BY BUS

If a cab hurtles you through a place and the Tube lets you bypass it completely, London's double-deckers show you the city from a whole new angle. Climb skyward to the second level (be sure to hold on), take a deep breath, relax, and enjoy watching the scenery from high above. The routes are by nature slow and circuitous and the sunlit second level warm and sleepy. In many ways, it's the perfect place to pause, nod off for a moment, or let your thoughts wander.

From this angle you really can see things that you wouldn't see otherwise, as most of the architecture in London pays special attention to the second story. Ornamental cornices, elaborate fenestration, and signage present a world of detail you wouldn't get a chance to see any other way.

Each one of us is an **OBSERVER**, a **DINER**, a **SHOPPER**, and a **MINGLER**

OBSERVER

Are you into architecture and culture but deep down really prefer people-watching?

Chelsea Physic Garden | 1

Dinosaur Hall: Natural History Museum | 2

The Great Court: British Museum | 3

Hackney City Farm | 4

Miller's Academy | 5

[MORE]

Mouth That Roars Studio 23 | 6

Oxo Tower | 7

[ROOFTOPS]

The Photographers' Gallery | 8

The Temple | 9

Terence Conran: Bibendum & Bluebird | 10

Unilever Series: Tate Modern | 11

[BATHROOMS OF LONDON]

DINER

Are you a food connoisseur who occasionally enjoys the authentic greasy spoon?

SHOPPER

Are you excited to get the inside scoop on the latest indie movie, cut of meat, or comic?

Are you an adroit social navigator who can take a conversation in any direction?

MINGLER

87
Help Wanted
for more info
contact-
zeina@amoul.com
hm & Blues
FOYLES
for
BOOKS
shop

OBSERVER

Social behaviors, fleeting moments, and subtle details can be very inspirational once you tune in to them. It's really just a matter of getting out there and opening yourself up to it all. Ask yourself some questions in the process: Is this space being used in the way it was intended? How might it encourage social interaction or support privacy? Does it evoke emotion or elicit a response? Every experience is an opportunity to look at things in a new way and gain insight about something or someone. Even yourself.

1

DURING A TRIP TO JAMAICA, Hans Sloane (of Sloane Square fame) was the apocryphal discoverer of the recipe for hot chocolate. He sold it to Cadbury—the first step to amassing a rather large fortune. A statue of Sloane overlooks the garden.

CHELSEA PHYSIC GARDEN

CHELSEA | 66 Royal Hospital Road | **CHELSEAPHYSICGARDEN.CO.UK** | 020 7352 5646

Inspiration comes in many forms. For Will Rosenzweig, social entrepreneur and co-founder of The Republic of Tea, it manifests in the form of Britain's first garden of world medicine established by London's worshipful society of apothecaries in 1673. As luck would have it, we met Will just days before starting field research for this book. With 5,000 different plants, more than 330 years of botanical and medical history, and a recommendation from a guy who knows his stuff about herbs, we couldn't wait to get there. "Once you pass through the gate you find yourself fully immersed in a botanic sanctuary, surrounded by plants that matter—for they offer cures, tonics, and elixirs that lift the human spirit," Will explained. This working garden is where the British brought tea plants back from China to hybridize for their Indian tea estates in the 1700s and 1800s. "Some of the original glass houses are still intact, so when I visit the garden, I connect directly to some of the tea that I drink now," Will added. Wander the garden with an expert guide and see what aspect of this urban oasis inspires you.

EVERYONE KNOWS THAT DINOSAURS are a big draw for kids, but no one knows it better than the Natural History Museum. Check out the kiosk that highlights so many of the different places dinosaurs pop up in our culture and our imagination.

2

DINOSAUR HALL

NATURAL HISTORY MUSEUM KENSINGTON | 76-86 Cromwell Road | **NHM.AC.UK** | 020 7942 5000

Maybe it's being on equal footing with a dinosaur at the top of a tensile walkway—or the skillfully hung, lit, and shadowed skeletons themselves—but something about this exhibit takes you where few other exhibits do: up. Walking along the skeletal bridge gives you a little time to get comfortable with the idea that you are walking among such massive, powerful creatures. And it gives you a dino's-eye view of the humans walking around the exhibit below. The exhibit is an excellent example of what you can accomplish with shadows and light. In this case, dozens of shadows play back as countless oversized dinosaur legs and jaws lunge out of the darkness. All you have to do is watch the kids' reactions, as they wander through, to recognize that any dinosaur exhibit worth its weight in bones should balance science with goosebumps.

FOR A BIRD'S-EYE VIEW of the multiple ways this public/private space is being used, spy on the rows of white communal lunch tables from a perch on the grand staircase.

THE GREAT COURT

BRITISH MUSEUM **BLOOMSBURY** | Great Russell Street | **THEBRITISHMUSEUM.AC.UK** | 020 7323 8000

Perhaps the fact that most museums in London are free makes them particularly welcoming spaces. But there's no place quite as simple, unique, and inviting as the central court of the British Museum. For starters, the dome designed by Sir Norman Foster is an engineering and mathematical triumph, casting shelter as well as geometric patterns over the courtyard below. This gateway to the museum's crown jewel, the Reading Room, is a town square of sorts—a place to gather casually, meet up with friends, sprawl, sketch, sneak a kiss, or even take a quick snooze. The "indooring" of the court creates a park-like setting and permission for behaviors that typically don't fly in other enclosed public spaces. The light and height of the dome takes people beyond their normal comfort zone and extends an invitation to make the space their own. Watch for the body language of flirty teenagers on a school trip, or the guy desperately trying to concentrate on his paper rather than on the volume of the cell phone conversation going on behind him.

EXPERIENCE THE BEAUTY of community by way of a county fair, a barn dance, or some good ol' sheep-shearing.

HACKNEY CITY FARM

HACKNEY | 1a Goldsmiths Row | **HACKNEYCITYFARM.CO.UK** | 020 7729 6381

Sometimes you need to take something out of context to really see the beauty in it. Hackney City Farm has done just that. It would certainly still be captivating in a country setting, but to find this small, organic community farm in the middle of the city takes it to a different level. Step inside and trade in the hectic vibe of the urban surroundings for a peaceful, pastoral one, as you visit sheep in the meadow or pigs in the barn. Each discrete experience within this urban oasis teaches a small, quiet lesson, be it about the source of our food or what it means to be a part of a small, nurturing group of caring people. Formerly a derelict brewery, the farm, open to the public since 1986, is a great example of creativity and reinvention. Grab a bite to eat in the café, check out the community "farm board" for activities, or take your kids to an art class. Everyone is welcome. And by all means, enjoy some home-baked treats or farm-fresh eggs courtesy of the resident hens and ducks.

[*] **IF YOU DON'T WANT THE EVENING TO END,** make a night of it and book a room at Miller's Residence, just down the street at 111a Westbourne Grove.

MILLER'S ACADEMY

NOTTING HILL | 28a Hereford Road | **MILLERSACADEMY.CO.UK** | 020 7229 5103

Martin Miller, an eclectic work of art in his own right, is a celebrated author, antiques expert, gin maker, and innkeeper who has recently added yet another colorful feather to his cap with Miller's Academy of Arts and Science. Tucked on a side street in Notting Hill, this members' club is a charming and quirky venue for lectures and lively debate—the perfect backdrop for an evening you won't soon forget. Speakers range from Chomsky scholars to former Russian spies. The evening we attended was part lecture, part book club, part *Jerry Springer Show*. But don't let that scare you—we mean it in a good way. The speaker was a chef turned dominatrix turned writer. (Intimate topics can make for lively discussions.) The salon itself had a role to play— surreal, colorful, and dreamlike. The membership quality gave the experience a sense of exclusivity and community. The scale was welcoming yet intimate—only sixty people per lecture, so plan ahead. Martin Miller's expertise in antiques and Victoriana manifest playfully throughout. This is a place to learn about serious topics, without taking them, or yourself, too seriously.

MORE

Whether it's the drag-queen's-garage-sale-esque quality of Lounge Lover in Shoreditch or the bejeweled stuffed animals who watch you dine at Les Trois Garçons just around the corner, supper in Gaudí's Sacre Coeur–like excess at Beach Blanket Babylon, or every choreographed inch of Miller's Residences in Notting Hill, London has a thing for things. And lots of them. We all know how the saying goes, but in this case, more is definitely more. After all, Victorian England invented excess with a piece of furniture or a bauble for every spare spot. Perhaps that's why the Brits bring it off with aplomb. It doesn't matter if these decorative collections are created from antiques or found objects, they mirror the complexity of life just the same. And for one reason or another, there's something comforting in the chaos of it all.

MTR
studio 23

MOST OF THE MOVIES AT MTR are made by the kids who use the studio downstairs, though other independent and documentary films are also available for viewing.

6

MOUTH THAT ROARS STUDIO 23

HOXTON | 23 Charlotte Road | **MOUTHTHATROARS.COM/MTRSTUDIO23.PHP** | 020 7729 2323

This is a great example of how a public space can feel private. At first glance, this is a place where you and a buddy can sit in a pair of airline seats and watch a film while listening on headsets. Odd yet compelling. The second time we visited, we inquired about the idea behind it all, and that's when things really got interesting. Mouth That Roars (MTR) is a nonprofit dedicated to giving kids a voice. Hence the formation of MTR Studio 23, a TV, documentary, and filmmaking studio that gives marginalized youth a platform while giving the public a unique opportunity to access their films and understand their lives. These kids are too frequently ignored, disrespected, or misrepresented by the media. MTR reminds them that their dreams, fears, and thoughts matter and that someone is listening. The concept behind this nonprofit is a powerful one. Grab some popcorn, a pair of headphones, and a movie off of the rack on the wall and see what these storytellers have to share.

ANTICIPATION CAN BE AN EXPERIENCE IN AND OF ITSELF. Enjoy the moments leading up to the opening of the elevator doors as you enter the restaurant or the bar.

7

OXO TOWER

SOUTH BANK | Barge House Street | **OXOTOWER.CO.UK** | 020 7803 3888

Why does St. Paul's Cathedral look so right from this angle, illuminated beneath the night sky? Our childhood visions of London aren't of crowded streetscapes, but, rather, of the open vista of rooftops and chimneys in *Mary Poppins* or of Peter Pan and Tinkerbell flitting about outside Wendy's window. Maybe that's why dinner in the restaurant atop the Oxo Tower seems so exciting yet familiar, dramatic yet comforting. It was a little too chilly to dine alfresco when we were there, but if you catch it at the right time of the year, you might just get lucky. Or sit inside under velvety blue light and watch a sunset or a storm rolling through.

ROOFTOPS

Good for Harvey Nichols for capturing all of the really great rooftops of London, whether serving brunch among the chimneys on the fifth-floor Foodmarket [16] in its Knightsbridge flagship store or capturing the glamorous sweep of the city from the windows of their restaurant and brasserie in the Oxo Tower [7]. Rooftops of London have a romanticism all their own, much like Harvey Nichols' brand and product packaging that tells a hell of a tale without so much as a word. These rooftop settings also speak volumes, creating just the right setting for your next story.

GREAT PHOTOGRAPHY makes you see things in ways you didn't think to see them before.

8

THE PHOTOGRAPHERS' GALLERY

SOHO | 5 & 8 Great Newport Street | **PHOTONET.ORG.UK** | 020 7831 1772

Part gallery, part bookshop, part café where you can snack while sitting in the middle of an exhibit, this gallery with two addresses on Great Newport Street is an inspiring place to go to rediscover photography and make you feel better about being a tourist with camera in hand. If you didn't bring your own, you can buy a Polaroid or a Holga in the bookstore, which itself feels like a gallery: the art is displayed in a thorough and engaging collection of photography books. Some believe that viewing the world from behind the lens of a camera feels distancing. The resulting images at this gallery feel anything but. We saw an exhibit made up of a collection of hundreds of found and faded family photos. They were organized by topic: backyard barbecues, a day at the beach, playing with pets. This spectrum of events faded effortlessly from one to the next, creating an experiential mind map. It was a lesson in memory, organization, and the art of the visual story.

The Porters & Police
have orders to remove
all persons making
a noise or creating
a disturbance
within this inn.

J. R. Hill
Under Treasurer

WE WERE BROUGHT HERE on a personal tour by Londoner and historian Clive Cheesman, a.k.a. Rouge Dragon Pursuivant at the College of Arms—which, by the way, we think is the coolest title on Earth.

6

THE TEMPLE

CITY OF LONDON | Middle Temple Lane | **MIDDLETEMPLE.ORG.UK** | 020 7427 4800

The Temple sits at the edge of the City of London, meaning the one square mile where London was born. It is an intricately variegated area, despite its relatively small size. While we were strolling with Clive, he told us, "If I walk more than a hundred yards in any direction, it feels like I've gone somewhere exotic. The trade of an area often dictates its personality. And within the City, you feel it more than you do in most places." There is a sudden shift from bankers to barristers as you leave Fleet Street and enter the realm of the Temple. Long ago, this was home to a medieval order of religious knights. Today it's filled with barristers and their offices. Neither streets nor squares, the space between buildings is public and meandering, though it is a members' club of sorts. Or at least, it feels that way. Well-dressed men in blue suits abound. We found ourselves standing a little taller. Speaking a bit more quietly. Treading lightly. Respectful visitors in a foreign land.

[*] **CHECK OUT THE BOOK** *Terence Conran on London* for a personal tour of the town, led by one of its greatest admirers and influencers.

TERENCE CONRAN

BIBENDUM **CHELSEA** | Michelin House, 81 Fulham Road | **BIBENDUM.CO.UK** | 020 7581 5817
BLUEBIRD **CHELSEA** | 350 King's Road | **BLUEBIRD-RESTAURANT.COM** | 020 7559 1000

If you look through the eyes of Sir Terence Conran, the world looks pretty good. His books on living in small homes make the cramped look charming, his restaurants favor comfort and refinement over all else, and his mixed-use spaces (Bibendum and Bluebird, for example) are revisions of London that nod to the past while stepping boldly into the present. Even his most surprising juxtapositions create sense and order. In fact, so much of modern experience in London is influenced by Conran's vision that it might be hard, at first, to see what's new or different about it. But then, the big idea here has always been about relevance rather than revelation.

11

UNILEVER SERIES

TATE MODERN **SOUTHWARK** | Turbine Hall, 53 Bankside | **TATE.ORG.UK/MODERN** | 020 7887 8888

The series of art works commissioned and installed in the Great Turbine Hall over the last seven years has consistently pushed the notion of art into spectacle and spectacle into pure physical and sensorial impact—sweaty palms and all. Whether it's the creaky, terrifying towers of the first Louise Bourgeois installation or the two-to-four-story corkscrew slides created by Carsten Höller that fill the hall with joyful screams, the work is always huge and awe-inspiring, inviting you to appreciate it first on a physical and emotional level and then on an intellectual level. The contributing artists play with scale, physicality, and approachability. The art isn't complete without interaction. However one chooses to engage it, this series requires you to get involved, in essence becoming a living, breathing part of the exhibit itself. The experience confronts your boundaries, not unlike dining at Dans le Noir? [15]—though instead of taking one of your senses away, the Unilever Series often turns up the volume on all of them at once. Enjoy the ride.

BATHROOMS OF LONDON

Any designer knows that it's the little things that prove the mettle of the craftsman, from how a pocket lining feels on a coat to the quality of endpapers in a book; these are the telling design details that test the fullness of a concept. London restaurateurs have done with bathrooms what Paul Smith [37] did with linings by realizing that these surprising details test, or at least complement, the experience. Whether it's the front-seat view of the whooshing trains from the bathroom windows at Smith's of Smithfield or the candid camera–esque feeling you get when mingling between the sexes at the stone sinks at Busaba in Soho, someone's paying attention to detail so others can have surprising interactions in the most unexpected of places.

DINER

We're not particularly discriminating when it comes to food—we like it all: the fried and the fresh, the processed and the pristine. What we are more interested in is the culture and behaviors that sprout up around a meal. The thrill of a great dining adventure comes not from the food alone but also from the service, the companions, and the environment. Observing how the parts of this whole overlap and come together often reveals the tastiest bits of all.

WE ASKED A LOCAL MERCHANT if there was anything in the area we should see. He pointed us toward the Warwick Avenue Tube station and said, "Go right on Formosa Street. You'll know when you get there."

AMOUL

MAIDA VALE | 14 Formosa Street | **AMOUL.COM** | 020 7286 6386

We found Amoul tucked between a flower shop and a design store. It's a small family-run deli with a big presence, despite having just a couple of tables and a handful of locals. We were enamored by the heavenly smells coming from the kitchen and the stories that graced the walls—black-and-white photos and handwritten quotes that set the tone for enjoying recipes passed down from generation to generation. Sustainable business practices including humane opening hours give Amoul Oakes the time and space to create everything from her signature Lebanese "brides" to licorice ice cream. Ever accommodating, she provides menus online a day ahead so you can place an order for pickup, turning what might seem like a limitation into a rather friendly gesture. The thing that really makes Amoul brilliant is its situation (location, location, location) at the crook of Formosa Street. No matter which end of the street you look down, Amoul is like a bracelet at the elbow, so perfect on such a perfect street that you feel as though you've walked onto a Hollywood set.

BATTLING BEIGELS OF BRICK LANE

BEIGEL BAKE **SHOREDITCH** | 159 Brick Lane | 020 7729 0826
BRITAINS FIRST & BEST BEIGEL SHOP **SHOREDITCH** | 155 Brick Lane | 020 7729 0616

Fresh-baked, warm beigels are a treat on their own, but pair them with salt beef and you've got one of the world's greatest Sunday hangover foods. The question is, what makes the clientele of these two virtually identical beigel shops, just one door down from each other, so loyal? Both are teeming with customers. How different can the beigels be? Do patrons ever try the place next door or do they stay true to one shop or the other? If so, why? Out of habit? Loyalty? A sense of community? On any given Sunday, you'll spot the crowds before you spot anything else. A constant stream of out-all-nighters and old-timers flows in and out, elbow to elbow, mouths watering, tummies happy. If you're visiting from across the pond, don't get your heart set on an American-style bagel. The spelling, consistency, and accompanying accoutrements are quite a bit different. Believe it or not, Londoners are about as passionate about these babies as New Yorkers. Let the best beigel/bagel win.

[✳] **FOR A FRESH TWIST** on the cupcake craze, head to Luna & Curious. This small, eclectic corner shop on Brick Lane (at Bacon Street) serves up T-shirt cupcakes in a tiny room at the back.

CRUMBS AND DOILIES

SUNDAY UP MARKET | Ely's Yard, The Old Truman Brewery | **CRUMBSANDDOILIES.CO.UK** | 077 7228 1457

Cupcakes are the new black. Seriously. They are everywhere. We loved them as kids and we love them just as much—if not more—now. So much so, the fact that boutique cupcake shops are popping up like Starbucks isn't the least bit annoying. It's supremely comforting. At Crumbs and Doilies in the Sunday Up Market **[49]**, it's also cute as can be. Beautiful bite-size cupcakes give new meaning to instant gratification. (Perhaps that's why dim sum and tapas are also enjoying a renaissance.) The proprietor takes it to the point of obsession, telling us, "I practically have carpal tunnel from decorating them from dawn to dusk." But we got the distinct impression she wouldn't have it any other way. Lucky for us.

IF A THREE-COURSE MEAL sounds a bit too daunting, you can go for a test run at happy hour.

DANS LE NOIR?

CLERKENWELL | 30–31 Clerkenwell Green | **DANSLENOIR.COM** | 020 7253 1100

Perhaps the most illuminating experience in the entire book, an evening at the restaurant Dans le Noir? is sure to alter the way you see the world—if only for an hour and a half. In retrospect, we're not sure what was most interesting: spending a night out with three colleagues in total darkness, observing how the group dynamic shifted after we lost our ability to see, or how we perceived the shift in our own behaviors individually. Not to mention trying to decipher what was on our plates (it's a surprise menu), having to rely entirely on hearing (challenging in a loud room), taste (disorienting when you don't know what's coming), and touch (we found ourselves using our fingers instead of utensils quite often). If you're not a fan of leaving your comfort zone, this probably isn't the experience for you. But if you're up for the ultimate empathy exercise, a tasty three-course meal, and an evening you won't soon forget, give Dans le Noir? a try. There are restaurants in Paris and in Moscow, too.

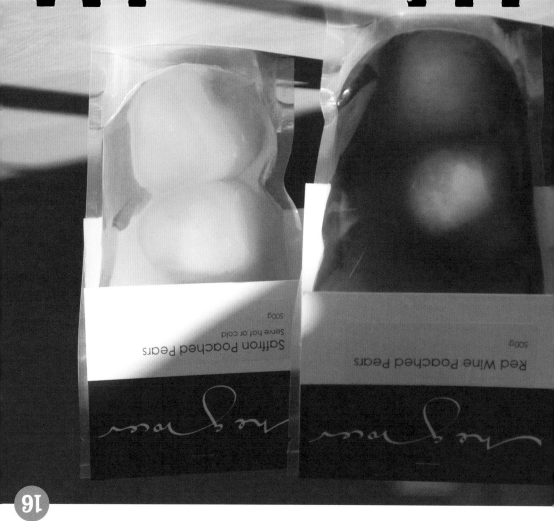

Saffron Poached Pears
Serve hot or cold
500g

Red Wine Poached Pears
500g

HARVEY NICHOLS FOODMARKET

KNIGHTSBRIDGE | 109–125 Knightsbridge | **HARVEYNICHOLS.COM** | 020 7235 5000
THE GROCER ON ELGIN **NOTTING HILL** | 6 Elgin Crescent | **THEGROCERON.COM** | 020 7437 7776

We are quite interested in the role storytelling plays in the world—particularly when the story is best told without words. Two of our faves fall into the category of packaging design. Harvey Nichols' own line of packaged foods—bedecked in grey, black, and silver images—plays perfectly with nostalgia and emotion. The Foodmarket on the fifth floor at Harvey Nichols' flagship store in Knightsbridge is one of our favorite spots for brunch and browsing the aisles. The Grocer on Elgin takes a completely different but equally elegant tack, with its let-the-food-speak-for-itself take on tempting the palate. Each of the pre-packaged meals is art unto itself, with the food taking center stage. Two poached pears in a plastic bag never looked so utterly perfect.

COURGETTE,
PEPPERS,
CARAMELIZED ONION
& BASIL £2.90

ALL THREE OTTOLENGHI LOCATIONS—in Notting Hill, Kensington, and Islington—are managed by different chefs serving different foods with different concepts.

OTTOLENGHI

NOTTING HILL | 63 Ledbury Road | **OTTOLENGHI.CO.UK** | 020 7727 1121

All of Notting Hill feels light, white, and ethereal, and this teensy lunch spot seems to have captured that and pushed it to its extreme. You can always get food to go, but we recommend heading straight to the back and soaking up some sun at the intimate communal table in Ottolenghi's original Ledbury Road location. Getting a seat feels a little bit like hitting the lottery—okay a small lottery. The space is so intimate—about the size of a queen bed—that you inevitably have to ask someone to get up from her seat so you can squeeze in. But instead of it feeling like a bother, it feels more like an opportunity to bond with the other lottery winners—if only for a moment. The all-white interior, skylight, and giant mirror at the far end of the room help create airiness in a square footage that is anything but. Somehow, it doesn't feel as if everyone's listening in on each other's conversations. In fact, the space encourages the opposite—intimacy with your companion and utter visual solitude so you can delight in the vibrancy of the food, which provides a stunning bit of color, texture, and flavor.

CORNBREAD
95 p | 100 g

UNTO THIS LAST [88] has an entirely different story than St. John, but they do share one guiding principle: wasting nothing.

ST. JOHN

CLERKENWELL | 26 St. John Street | **STJOHNRESTAURANT.CO.UK** | 020 7251 0848

Known in London and beyond for having a "nose to tail" philosophy on food, St. John, cleverly located around the corner from the famed Smithfield (meat) Market, lets as little as possible slip past your plate. And it seems St. John's carnivorous followers believe the proprietors are onto something. In fact, chef Fergus Henderson has penned two books on the subject. And with his partner, restaurateur Trevor Gulliver, St. John expanded, opening another restaurant, bakery, and wine company in Spitalfields a few years back. The aesthetic at St. John is clean. The white, open, spare space is weighted gently with delicate black accents. Henderson's books carry the same aesthetic. Interestingly, in a restaurant that's all about making the most of every morsel of meat, St. John strikes a balance with a backdrop that utilizes as little as possible.

GET LOST IN THE SCENOGRAPHY of it all—a stage well set for an experience well worth having.

STORY DELI

SHOREDITCH | 3 Dray Walk, The Old Truman Brewery, 91 Brick Lane | 020 7247 3137

Story Deli has the most amazing communal table in town, and its organic pizza—and organic everything else—is insane. The magic happens in one perfect room with a glass wall street-side so everyone outside can see what they're missing. This find on Dray Walk, around the corner from Sunday Up Market **[49]**, is worth fighting the crowds for. The place is about total disclosure, physically and ideologically. It's also about bringing festivity to food, particularly on a weekend if you're able to snag a spot at one of the picnic tables outside on the Lane. The sincerity inside spills out to the street and captivates many a passerby. We were no exception. Scale, once again, plays an important role. The intimacy of the space and the humility of the materials all around you make you feel like you've been there before and that the moment was created just for you. Story Deli creates the perfect haven from the hustle and bustle of city life.

COMMUNAL TABLES

Something big has hit London—great, big, friendly communal tables. Is it nostalgia for the school refectory or is it really just that everybody's looking for the chance to come out from me-focused hibernation and hang with their neighbors? Some places in London are practically defined by great communal tables (Story Deli [19] or Monmouth Coffee Company [46]). Some provide them as a solution to size constraints. Whatever the impetus, sitting at a two-top feels a tad lonesome these days. There's just something so comforting about bellying up to a big, wooden farm table. Plus, it gives permission to the solo diner/tea drinker/happy hour–goer to be a part of it all. Communal tables are one of our favorite spots for observing public/private behaviors; it's an opportunity to see multiple behaviors play out on one stage. And hey, let's face it, it's a nice way to meet someone new, too.

IT'S NOT SURPRISING that Jules Wright, the woman behind The Wapping Project, has a background in theatrical lighting, as drama is at the foundation of this fairy tale.

THE WAPPING PROJECT

WAPPING | Wapping Hydraulic Power Station | **THEWAPPINGPROJECT.COM** | 020 7680 2080

This former hydraulic power plant turned gallery/restaurant/bar hybrid is, by design, a work in progress, though you'd never guess. Every touch feels deliberate, weighty, and purposeful. Pushing adaptive reuse to its furthest limit, it takes a special kind of eye to see how to make such an industrial place feel so warm and intimate—right down to the heated floors. The service seems to compensate for the intensity of the space with a familial casualness that complements the experience nicely. There are many interesting nooks and crannies throughout—from the pillar candles dripping unapologetically down windowsills and old hydraulic equipment, to the rooftop deck replete with water views. The most surprising space of all, however, is the gallery. Take a gander between courses. Marvel at the poetry of a perfectly lit room. Contemplate the previous life of this gracious building. But above all, be sure to come back again soon to appreciate the ever-changing character of this dramatic space.

LEGACY CAN BE a powerful experiential component if given just the right touch. As with most things, there is a fine line between striking the perfect chord and creating dissonance. The Wolseley is definitely an example of the former.

THE WOLSELEY

ST. JAMES | 160 Piccadilly | **THEWOLSELEY.COM** | 020 7499 6996

The history of a place alone can create the kind of ambience and experience you'll never forget. Combine that with an exquisite structure and you've got The Wolseley, a bank turned luxury car showroom turned elegant restaurant. You can't help but mind your manners while sipping champagne inside this gilded cage. While other places may be haunted by headless queens, this one is haunted by money, and lots of it. Have a glass of bubbly in the old vault (now the bar), gaze across the massive stone expanse, and you just might catch a glimpse of some big spenders of the past.

TRACES OF THE PAST

Walk through St. John's Square in Clerkenwell, and watch as others skitter by on their way to work or to the local gastropub (think pints plus great food). In particular, note the foundation path in the square, which traces an arc of a building that stood there long ago. Some passersby are so focused on the day's tasks that this relic doesn't seem to register for them. But others honor its memory by walking its course. It can be very seductive to follow a route set by others who have gone before you, be it footsteps in the sand or a hopscotch grid chalked out on the pavement. (Hopscotch itself is a trace of the past, invented in ancient Britain during the early Roman Empire.) There are subtle and not-so-subtle physical reminders of history all across London. This layering of past and present has a palpable presence throughout the city and takes on a character of its own. Each remnant reminds us that one day we too may create a path that others wander down or find inspiring.

SHOPPER

Shopping is one of our favorite ways to see the world. For some, a great sense of satisfaction comes from finding that perfect thing. For others, the quest itself is enough. The way we shop and where we shop say a lot about us, and retailers know it. A great deal of thought and energy go into the entire experience, from catching our eye to enticing us to buy. Like it or not, some of the most interesting and delightful experiences out there emerge from the minds of retailers big and small.

21a

MR. BINKS WANDERED into the shop in 1921 and has been its beloved mascot ever since.

BATES GENTLEMEN'S HATTER

ST JAMES | 21a Jermyn Street | **BATES-HATS.CO.UK** | 020 7734 2722

If James Smith & Sons **[31]** makes you feel like you've stepped into a museum, Bates Gentlemen's Hatter makes you feel like you've stepped back in time and into a closet. Not your closet. Somebody else's. Which brings all the discomfort that might suggest. This dark, mysterious space—stacked floor to ceiling with hatboxes, hats, and caps from all eras—has a Dickensian feel you're unlikely to find anywhere else. Perhaps it's the milliner who works to the sound of a great ticking clock, or the stuffed, top-hat-wearing cat, Mr. Binks, keeping watch over things. If you are brave enough to walk to the back of the store and ask for assistance, no doubt you will walk out of the shop with the best-fitting, best-made hat you've ever owned.

"**BETWEEN DOG AND WOLF**" is a crude translation of the old French expression, *entre chien et le loup*, meaning twilight—Charlotte's favorite time of the day.

BETWEEN DOG & WOLF

TOWER HAMLETS | 130 Columbia Road | **BETWEENDOGANDWOLF.COM** | 079 6141 5460

There's a lot to be thankful for on Columbia Road, including Charlotte van Cuylenburg, the proprietor of a charming shop that would make any gardener swoon. Matte black walls give the statuesque table in the middle of the room prominence. Bearing nothing but a neat grid of gifts, books, and tools, it commands a powerful presence—a kind of runway for curated objects. The placement of the table and everything on it creates an experiential vortex that draws you in and around it. Just the right amount of wares presented in a perfect patchwork can create order out of what's on offer. If you squint real hard, the blanket-strewn street sales happening down the road on Brick Lane or up in Camden Town take a similar tack. Between Dog & Wolf has a curious collection of items at first glance, particularly the wine rack tucked into one wall. "For people who like to drink while gardening?" we asked. Not quite. "Everything from growing the vines to drinking the wines," Charlotte clarified. And you can get in on the fun, too. Come to a wine-tasting evening and you may get a chance to help choose next season's selection.

WHAT GOES BEST with a bookstore dedicated to cooking? A café where chefs can come and prepare the fare that inspires them.

BOOKS FOR COOKS

NOTTING HILL | 4 Blenheim Crescent | **BOOKSFORCOOKS.COM** | 020 7221 1992

You know how you should never go food shopping when you're hungry? Well, it turns out the same holds true with browsing cookbooks before lunch. There's nothing like the smell of a little garlic sautéing in a pan to get you in the mood to buy a cookbook or ten. Books for Cooks is exactly what it sounds like, but its name doesn't reveal all, making a trip to the shop quite a treat. There's a sun-filled test kitchen in back where chefs are trying out their latest inspirations and giving cookery demonstrations. And guess who gets to enjoy the fruits of their labors? Peruse the cork board in back to learn more about the kinds of people chefs like doing business with—such as Sheepdrove Organic Farm Family Butchers in Bristol. This and other must-know local purveyors put you at the center of a homespun, casual world of cooking—London-style.

STROLL ON OVER to the intersection of Ezra & Columbia **[44]**, and celebrate your flower finds with oysters on the half-shell or a great big wedge of artisan cheese.

COLUMBIA ROAD FLOWER MARKET

TOWER HAMLETS | Columbia Road | **COLUMBIA-FLOWER-MARKET.FREEWEBSPACE.COM**

Walk toward the market from virtually any direction and you'll see a steady parade of people carrying flats of daffodils and bundles of cherry blossom branches. As a shop owner at nearby Broadway Market told us, "Walking into Columbia Market on Sunday is like finding a jungle in the middle of the city." You know you've arrived when you hear the symphony of flower sellers vying for attention with deals that get better as the day goes on. Things can get rather crowded here, but the crowd is friendly amidst the fragrance of fresh flowers. Don't forget to pop into some of the wonderful independent shops such as Between Dog & Wolf [23] or Labour and Wait [33]—a nice complement and tribute to the flowers out front.

GO ON AN ADVENTURE in this bookstore geared toward travelers.

DAUNT BOOKS

MARYLEBONE | 83 Marylebone High Street | **DAUNTBOOKS.CO.UK** | 020 7224 2295

There is an art to displaying books—getting one to leap off a shelf without fighting for attention with the one next to it. But what we found even more interesting was that, beyond the books themselves, a room can be even more persuasive in encouraging the romance of reading. As we wandered toward the back of the store, we discovered an enchanting, two-story, sunlit reading room with long oak galleries—a bookworm's buried treasure tucked away inconspicuously on Marylebone High Street. The unfolding of the experience felt quite special, not unlike wandering upon a great passage in a book that grabs you by the lapels and takes you into another world for a while. This Edwardian-era bookshop stays true to its illustrious roots, specializing in travel, art, and beauty. If ever a room inspired readers of any age to appreciate books, this would be it. Unpretentious. Approachable. Inviting. Sun-drenched. Beautiful. Belle époque, indeed.

DAYLESFORD ORGANIC practices some of the most refined communication about organics that we've seen, making sustainability feel like anything but a sacrifice.

27

DAYLESFORD ORGANIC

MAIDA VALE | 5a Clifton Villas | **DAYLESFORDORGANIC.COM** | 020 7266 1932
CLIFTON NURSERIES MAIDA VALE | 5a Clifton Villas | **CLIFTON.CO.UK** | 020 7289 6851

A secret garden store in the middle of a secret garden tucked away on a secret little street. Or so it seems, as you slip between the gates that lead you to Clifton Nurseries. This hidden oasis in the middle of Little Venice is a treat unto itself, but coupled with two Daylesford Organic stores—one dedicated to organic food and the other to gardening—everything seems to fall perfectly into place. The explosion of floral color complements the neutral tones inside the stores. The small food shop filled with pristine packaged food is so white and well lit, you'll feel like you're grocery shopping in heaven. The garden store/café is equally impressive and will leave you contemplating the leather milk flask for your garden tea set for far longer than makes sense. Of course, all retail is about selection and authority, but Daylesford Organic is especially good at evoking a gracious garden lifestyle.

LOOK TO NATURE for the most beautiful color combinations. Unless you're in London. Then, by all means, look to Designers Guild.

DESIGNERS GUILD

CHELSEA | 267 & 277 King's Road | **DESIGNERSGUILD.COM** | 020 7351 5775

After a bite at Bluebird **[10]** or an afternoon of retail therapy, pop into Designers Guild for a little color therapy. This, Tricia Guild's flagship store on Kings Road, is the center of the colorist world. Though we all know that color matters and the shop has been around for years, it is still a relaxing and wonderful thing to happen into a place that reminds you of this so effortlessly. Tricia brings color front and center without overwhelming the senses. The effect, in fact, is rather soothing. The various rooms each celebrate a different color-tone with product assortments based on palette over practicality. Organization by color shows that something so simple can also be powerful.

IF YOUR EYES NEED A BREAK, Foyles' narrow jazz café fronting Charing Cross Road is the perfect place to catch your breath and feast your ears before heading back into the stacks.

FOYLES

SOHO | 113–119 Charing Cross Road | **FOYLES.CO.UK** | 020 7437 5660

Before Amazon.com, there had to be a place where all the books in the world were kept, and we'd like to think it was Foyles. With room after room of reading enjoyment, a place like this reminds you of the infiniteness of the universe. You'll find everything you could possibly dream of, plus a few things you'd prefer not to—we even stumbled upon a book on designing your own sitcom set. The distinctive neon sign out front is so recognizable that we suspect that it has turned Soho into a veritable brothel for books, which would explain mega-chains like Borders and Waterstone's across the road and several other small specialty bookstores scattered close by.

HAYVEND

COFFEE @ 157 **SHOREDITCH** | 157 Brick Lane | **HAYVEND.COM** | 077 4716 8759

For two pounds, a yellow vending machine on the wall beckons you to drop in your coins for an original piece of art from a local artist. Art. In a box. Signed. After slight technical difficulties—user failure—we succeeded at following the directions properly and pulling out the little black drawer that revealed our very own little yellow box. It was "Relaxing Sounds from the Modern World" by artist Samuel Williams. Snippets of sound bites taken while waiting to do something else. Oddly peaceful and comforting white noise. A mere sampling of several hour-long recordings of everything from a car ride to the ambient sounds of a basement apartment. A caffeinated beverage and a signed piece of art for less than five pounds? Make that two to go, please.

JAMES SMITH & SONS is the kind of place you've walked by a thousand times and always said you'd check out, but never have. Definitely do.

JAMES SMITH & SONS

BLOOMSBURY | 53 New Oxford Street | **JAMES-SMITH.CO.UK** | 020 7836 4731

Umbrellas are one of those things you can never have too many of (especially in London). A wonderful find on a rainy day, James Smith & Sons is equally worth the trip under blue skies. Established in 1830, and on its present site since 1857, the shop now sells "semiautomatic" umbrellas. (Some things change, some stay the same.) The pride of craftsmanship, confidence of quality, and genuine passion for helping you find just the right size, materials, features, and fit make you realize what an important role authenticity plays in being an authority. P.S. The umbrella we bought that day is one that we hope to never accidentally leave behind on a train or in a restaurant. But if we do, we hope you find it, and enjoy the beauty of something you might once have thought banal.

THE THING IS

When you walk into a shop that specializes in just one thing, you expect the people inside to really know their stuff. Or at least, that they should. Particularly when that shop has been in existence for decades, the art passed down through a family or shared by longtime business partners. Bates Gentlemen's Hatter [22] and James Smith & Sons [31] are two such examples of this sort of dedication and extreme expertise. The minute you walk inside, you know you are going to be well taken care of. This kind of craftsmanship encourages and inspires going deep into a field of knowledge and mastering it. There's an even deeper sense of satisfaction that comes from sharing it with others, which makes it gratifying to stand on either side of the glass counter. Teacher and student enter into an animated volley of give and take. A different kind of relationship is formed when interacting with the same people over the course of many years—even decades. It's all too rare these days in a world giving way to big box stores. So it's particularly nice to come across a place that puts its energy into the art of one thing, rather than stocking just about everything.

CONCEIVED AFTER FOUR FRIENDS showed up to a party in the same dress, Junky Styling ensures that will never happen to them—or you—again.

JUNKY STYLING

SHOREDITCH | 12 Dray Walk, The Old Truman Brewery, 91 Brick Lane | **JUNKYSTYLING.CO.UK** | 020 7247 1883

The things that typically wind up in the recycling bin aren't the only items that deserve a shot at a second life. Sure, anybody with a needle and thread these days seems to be trying their hand at transforming pre-worn items and American Apparel tees. But the gals at Junky Styling were talking about creative reuse ten years ago, and nobody does it better. Bring in a favorite piece of clothing whose cut just isn't cutting it anymore. Or peruse their collection of one-of-a-kind jackets, shirts, and skirts. Born of vintage or (gasp) generic beginnings, each hyper-engineered piece is art unto itself, styled in a way that doesn't take itself too seriously. From frayed or forgotten to bespoke and becoming, it's the most stylish take on recycling we've seen.

SIMPLY STEP OUT of Labour and Wait, onto the street at the top half of Brick Lane, and into the frenzy of the Sunday street market for a wholly different take on everyday items.

LABOUR AND WAIT

SHOREDITCH | 18 Cheshire Street | **LABOURANDWAIT.CO.UK** | 020 7729 6253

In the heart of East London's market district, this shop defines demure. Yes, this store focuses on functional design. Yes, they choose only to work with those who manufacture in traditional ways. Yes, the focus is on original designs, both new and vintage. And, as beautiful as all of that is, it doesn't come close to the beauty of the objects themselves. Measuring, boiling, trimming, tying, pouring, and sweeping have never looked more enticing. We assure you, you'll never look at a dustpan the same way again.

LONDON IS KNOWN FOR ITS THEATRE. And though there are no curtains or ushers or plush velvet seats from which to watch the performance, you get to be a part of it all at Liberty.

34

LIBERTY OF LONDON

SOHO | Great Marlborough Street | **LIBERTY.CO.UK** | 020 7734 1234

Walking through the front entrance of Liberty is like slipping through the back of a lush flower shop into the hidden kingdom of Narnia. This luxuriously upscale department store tucked inside a Tudor mansion will charm you if you give it the time it deserves. Any discerning individualist could easily spend half a day inside, exploring each delightfully choreographed detail. Liberty captures some of the best London has to offer, layering what feels like a trip to a theatre, museum, and boutique all in one. Exquisite fabrics and signature patterns are placed throughout the store with amazing finesse resulting in a crescendo of cohesion. Departments as diverse as knitting, chocolate, and tailoring peacefully and playfully coexist under one roof. Pop in and take a gander at what the women are working on in the knitting room—undoubtedly something bright and beautiful. Then top it all off with afternoon tea in a cozy little decoupage wonderland on the ground floor. Encore, encore.

NEAL'S YARD REMEDIES

COVENT GARDEN | 2 Neal's Yard | **NEALSYARDREMEDIES.COM** | 020 7379 7222

Neal's Yard Remedies comes from a place of tradition with a holistic bent on natural therapies and wellness. Its history along with its trademark apothecary packaging; the light, bright, come-on-in store design; and the earthbound staff make you feel better just being there, whether or not you book an hour in one of the therapy rooms. Humble beginnings and ethical intentions back in Covent Garden's bohemian Neal's Yard set the tone for the brand in 1981 and can still be felt in the stores today, on the Web site, in the language used, and in the materials—printed on chlorine-free recycled paper using vegetable inks, of course. Dried herbs, homeopathic remedies, essential oils, flower remedies, and a range of toiletries based on herbs and essential oils are displayed and described simply and with approachability in mind. Somehow, treatments like iridology and polarity therapy seem more approachable here, too, thanks to plain language and soothing graphics. When it comes to making people feel comfortable, there's something to be said for the art of simplicity.

NEWBURGH STREET

SOHO | Newburgh Street

Newburgh Street is where the big boys come to play on a smaller scale and try their hand at experimentalism. Mega-brands reinterpret themselves and speak to us in new ways. Adidas Originals features, among other things—you guessed it—original Adidas trainers from the '50s, '60s, and '70s on up. Cinch, owned by Levi's, feels like a gallery for vintage and designer denim. At the Fred Perry concept shop, select artists are invited to design limited edition shirts. 55DSL is the feel-at-home Diesel flagship for the street-wear set, all about making teens and twenty-somethings feel at home, complete with turntables, TV, well-worn furniture, and a fridge. The lithe and quirky Beyond the Valley is thrown in for a little local, small-shop design flavor. The bright-lights, big-city cousin to Exmouth Market **[43]**, Newburgh Street is catering to a very different kind of clientele. But a similar closed-system feel brings everything together in a very cohesive way.

PAUL SMITH IS A MASTER at something we call scenography—setting a scene that lets the consumer step in and become a part of the story.

PAUL SMITH

NOTTING HILL | 122 Kensington Park Road | **PAULSMITH.CO.UK** | 020 7727 3553

When does something ordinary become extraordinary? How can you make even the most mundane things sing? Well, for starters, you can walk into any Paul Smith store and start trying on clothes. Slip your hand into a pocket of a pair of jeans and see how surprising a silk lining feels when you were expecting down-and-dirty denim. Or pick up a shoe to find not just the size but also an artist's rendering of London's urban landscape on the sole. Little surprising details. Twists on that which we take for granted. Sometimes that's all it takes to coax a smile or make you feel like you've been given the secret word of the day, letting you in on a world that others haven't yet found. Smith creates visual and experiential vignettes within every room in his various shops, each begging you to step farther inside. It's an investment that is sure to bring a joyful return. Like Terence Conran **[10]**, Paul Smith has forged his own eclectic way across London and beyond, pioneering and redefining so many elements of the retail experience along the way, it's hard to picture things without him.

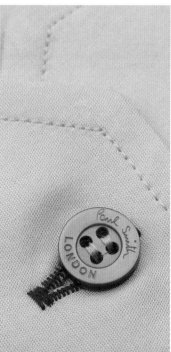

GLORIFYING THE EVERYDAY

There are some things most of us just don't think about as design inspiration. Things we use day in and day out without thinking twice—a teakettle, a toothbrush, a wallet, a waste bin. Others of us thrive on the idea of evoking delight in someone's day—particularly when they least expect it. Two of the great design challenges we face are overcoming the ubiquity of everyday objects, and the sheer bounty of items we use, wear, rely on, and wonder how we ever did without. Looking at "usual" things in an unusual way and designing with delight as an end goal invites us to transcend our expectations and take a moment to reflect on our ability to find inspiration in even the most unlikely places. Inspiration: It's free, it doesn't discriminate, it's available 24/7, and doing something with it just might brighten someone's day.

THESE GENTS borrowed the name of their store from the title of a book written in 1860 by John Ruskin. The author advocated a return to the local craftsman's workshop, right when the Industrial Revolution was raging.

UNTO THIS LAST

SHOREDITCH | 230 Brick Lane | **UNTOTHISLAST.CO.UK** | 020 7613 0882

Unto This Last is an excellent model for sustainable business practices and a great example of a symbiotic relationship between old-world craftsmanship and computer-generated methodologies. These guys harness technology to play a meaningful role in the re-creation of local, distributed manufacturing. While you shop, you can also watch the craftsmen at work on computer-guided machinery in the back, where they manufacture absolutely everything they sell—which means no need for warehousing, transportation, or packaging. Even though everything is made to order (within five days, mind you), they are able to keep their costs competitive with mass-production prices. It's a great example of how seeing the source makes something more special and, in this case, more economical. They'll even show you the patterned sheets of plywood used for your new table so you can see how much, or rather how little, waste there was. The leftover bits become funky little coasters or can't-live-without-'em candleholders.

WASTE NOT

Whether we're talking about food or furniture, craftsmen or chefs, people are feeling passionate about "doing the right thing." The local thing. The authentic thing. The least wasteful thing. It's a get-back-to-basics mentality that is rewarded by more than just the benefits of good business practices. This "new" source of creativity and inspiration is resonating with consumers. And, it's enjoying a growing renaissance that doesn't look like it's going away anytime soon. In fact, quite the opposite. It's a cross-cultural, cross-industry concept that has begun to manifest in meaningful ways. Finally, a comprehensible way to communicate the virtues of sustainability to the masses.

MINGLER

If one is good, two is better, and it only gets more interesting the more you add. Experiences that support groups of people or, more importantly, those that encourage meeting are especially intriguing to us. Some of the most sophisticated experiences aren't great at inspiring social connection, while some of the least designed interactions are the most successful. If you're going exploring, it's almost always more fun with a sidekick or two.

SWAP FINGERS FOR FORKS and church walls for white tablecloths and head upstairs to Roast for a savory sit-down [*] while peering at the market below.

BOROUGH MARKET

SOUTHWARK | 8 Southwark Street | **BOROUGHMARKET.ORG.UK** | 020 7407 1002

Under the roar of the train tracks, wedged between Southwark Cathedral and a knot of quaint streets lined with stylish shops, Borough Market lets you rethink your notion of street food. Twenty centuries old (250 years in this very location), it doesn't look any worse for wear. It's thriving more than ever in the midst of the latest culinary renaissance. This bustling maze of a market will make you think that eating while perching, squatting, or leaning huddled in groups of two or four against churchyard fences is the way meals were meant to be had. In addition to being the center of all things gastronomic in London, most of the stalls here have perfected the notion of two-handed servings, whether salt-beef sandwiches, savory pies, or falafel wraps. Just because you're busy devouring some tasty morsel doesn't mean you can't be scouting your next snack.

THE TEAM BEHIND CAFÉ KICK traveled the globe to find the best that foosball has to offer. It seems they found what they were looking for.

CAFÉ KICK

CLERKENWELL | 43 Exmouth Market | **CAFEKICK.CO.UK** | 020 7837 8077

There's a unity that comes from competing with like-minded enthusiasts. Foosball is one of those rare things that crosses cultures and bonds people together. Whether you've spent some serious time at the tables or prefer to observe, you'll appreciate the neighborly vibe at Café Kick. To play, challenge the winner of the last match. It's a great way to meet people from all over the world and learn new rules and customs (foosball has a whole host of rules that players faithfully follow). Most take the game quite seriously, but everyone is welcoming—and a wee bit competitive. Enjoy playing on French Bonzini tables with beech wood, cast-iron figurines, and proper World Cup cork balls. (It seems the patrons aren't the only ones who take the game seriously.) Inside and out, this place is charming, but not "pub" charming. It feels more like being transported to a small town in Italy or France.

LIKE THE GROCER ON ELGIN [16], Coffee@ has captured the essence of personalization and translated it for each location.

COFFEE@157

SHOREDITCH | 157 Brick Lane | 020 7729 2666

We visited Coffee@157 on Brick Lane. It's a small chain, but the simple naming convention ties each coffee shop to its location. Casual language, community boards, witty furnishings (check out the to-go cup light fixtures), free Wi-Fi, and the art-dispensing machine by the door make the place feel more local than not. If *ReadyMade* were a coffee shop, it would be Coffee@. The décor and the coffee crowd alike have a certain DIY vibe. And the nomenclature will allow this small chain to continue to feel local, connected, and true to its roots, even as it grows. So far so good: Each time we walked by or went in, the place was packed. Once, we ended up by the door, trying to decide whether to stick around or go. That's when the Hayvend box **[30]** caught our eye.

joy private pre- or post-show drinks and dining as well as other privileges—such as first dibs on

ELECTRIC CINEMA

NOTTING HILL | 191 Portobello Road | **ELECTRICCINEMA.CO.UK** | 020 7908 9696

Members' clubs are popping up all over cities like London and New York. Who says a casual night at the movies can't feel a little exclusive? This is a great example of how a subtle rethinking of a set of experiences can result in a delightful shift in expectations. Going to the movies, munching on popcorn, watching previews and the feature presentation. It's fairly predictable, right? Not true at Electric Cinema. Movie-going is turned into the perfect night out with a simple reinterpretation of the rituals of eating, seating, previewing, and joining. Enjoy a bottle of wine and light fare right from the comfort of your very comfy (assigned) seat, or have an ice-cream sundae if that's more your style. Watch the screen as it "grows" in size and adds to the anticipation of what's to come, including a short piece on the rich history of the cinema. You'll want to buy your tickets ahead of time. We venture a guess that members get the best seats, but truly, there isn't a bad seat in the house.

A SENSE OF BELONGING

London is no stranger to the concept of exclusivity and membership. It may look and feel different now than it did back in the day, but at heart, it's still all about feeling like you belong—and being okay with the fact that others might not. We're not talking Dark Age stuff like discrimination based on sex, creed, or color. We are talking about people with above-average affluence, though. Upscale movie theatres with membership privileges. Hotels that require you to write an essay before being considered. Restaurants and bars with secret rooms—an inner sanctum for the precious few. Supper clubs that stake a claim for a month or so and then disappear once they've been "found out" by the public. We desperately tried to find a private writers' club we'd heard about, but to no avail, despite the fact that someone at IDEO actually belongs to it. (He gets points for his writerly allegiances.) It's human nature to want to feel like you're a part of something. In this case, it just happens to come with a price tag.

EXMOUTH MARKET

CLERKENWELL | Exmouth Market | **EXMOUTHMARKET.CO.UK**

Wander through Exmouth Market in the center of Clerkenwell and find yourself in a wonderfully village-esque setting just a stone's throw from busy Farringdon Road. This charming spot has its own microclimate, made up of just the right combination of eateries, bakeries, shops, and pubs—including a farmers' market on Fridays and Saturdays. Everything about this place oozes charm and authenticity. Small local businesses prevail and play off of each other with the greatest of ease, contributing heartily to the natural ecology. It's the kind of place where people learn each other's names and you want to stick around so they'll learn yours, too. Day or night, you can string together a combination of experiences that speak to you. Depending on time of day, it can offer very different vibes. Come on a weekday morning and pick up pastries among the focused work crowd. Come after dark on a Friday or Saturday night and stroll leisurely along under a canopy of white lights, and pretend you're somewhere far from London.

FOR A DIFFERENT TAKE ON TIME, drive by The Tea Building at 56 Shoreditch High Street. Looming light over its front door is a digital clock that continually counts down to last call seven nights a week.

EZRA & COLUMBIA

TOWER HAMLETS | Ezra Street at Columbia Road
JONES DAIRY **TOWER HAMLETS** | 23 Ezra Street | **JONESDAIRY.CO.UK** | 020 7739 5372

Now you see it, now you don't. This tiny, time-based intersection is our favorite brunch spot in town, hands down. That is, if you don't mind sitting on a curb rather than a chair. Depending on when you happen upon this intersection, you will either experience some serious alfresco snacking or find yourself on a deserted cobblestone street. Jones Dairy sits right in the middle at 23 Ezra, in case you need a landmark to help you find this find. Arrive before 2 pm on a Sunday, and you'll see lots of people and their pets taking to the streets—sitting, perching, or standing while enjoying oysters, coffee, cheeses, and breads. Each specialty shop, all within steps of one another, opens for a few hours until it has sold out of the day's goods. By "shop," we mean painted wooden doors and windows that open onto the street during "business hours." You'll see lots of flowers tucked under people's arms, freshly liberated from the Columbia Road Flower Market **[25]**. It doesn't get any more local than this.

HERE TODAY

Half the fun of having fun is about discovery. So it's no wonder that experiences that change over time are naturally appealing. Take, for example, the myriad markets in London that are only open one or two days a week. If you accidentally miss one, you feel a sense of loss. But when you hit it on the right day at the right time, it can be supremely satisfying. Even when bars shut themselves in after 11 pm, it creates a different kind of atmosphere than just an hour earlier. Other places, like Hoxton Square after hours, attract behavior that was never intended. At dark, the gate that surrounds it is locked to keep people out of the park. But the twenty-somethings frequenting the bars along the perimeter prefer to interpret "keep out" as "come in." Despite the obvious intention that goes along with a locked public space, large groups of people jump the (rather tall) fence and enjoy their anarchy along with their favorite beverages. Which brings us to those few hours between last call and when the street sweeper appears—trash in the gutters an abstract portrait of events the night before.

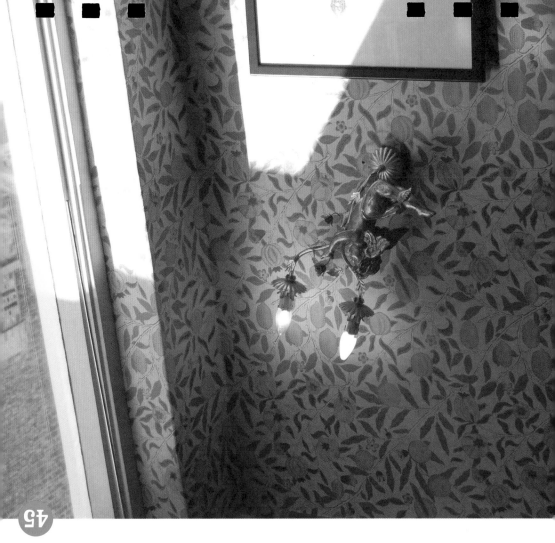

IF YOU CAN'T GET IN to Kandy Tea Room, there's an Ottolenghi take-out window [17] directly across the street.

KANDY TEA ROOM

KENSINGTON | 4 Holland Street | 020 7937 3001

We asked a woman working in a shop in Knightsbridge about this place, and she lit up and said, "I've always wanted to go." Now having been ourselves, we understand why. No more than eight tables are tucked into this tiny Sri Lankan–run tea room. The walls are adorned with an unlikely combination of photos of the owner's family, the royal family, cupids, Buddhas, and Crayola-drawn cows. If the tables are filled, there's no wait list to sign or queue to stand in. You're just politely turned away. After all, no one can really say how long tea will last. And (we're guessing) it would be impolite to hover around and make those seated feel rushed while enjoying afternoon tea and sandwiches. The tea room's motto is "nice tea for nice people." And whether it's the power of suggestion, or the fact that only really nice people frequent Kandy Tea Room, we couldn't have had a nicer time.

TEA TIME

Whether at The Ritz, Kandy Tea Room [45], or Liberty of London [34], everyone puts their mark on this special meal where gossip and gastronomy merge. All of the paraphernalia, from silver tea-strainers and three-tier trays right down to the white linen napkin folded neatly in your lap, contribute to a sense of ritual. Tea can be tied to time of day, an afternoon meal, or just a really great excuse to connect meaningfully with someone. Along with this ritual comes an intimacy and a heightened level of awareness. While some might assume tea behavior is all about uplifted pinkies, politeness, and pretension, everywhere we went, it seemed everyone was really enjoying themselves, each other, and everything on their plates.

BREAD and JAM
£2.50 per person
Please pay at the till.
Thank You

WHOLE BEAN COFFEE is delivered daily from Monmouth's roasting facilities in Covent Garden.

MONMOUTH COFFEE COMPANY

SOUTHWARK | 2 Park Street | **MONMOUTHCOFFEE.CO.UK** | 020 7645 3585

Like Amoul [12] on Formosa Street in Maida Vale, the Monmouth Coffee Company across from Borough Market certainly has location going for it—and a lot more. This coffee shop has a dedicated cult following. And why not? It's the perfect place to enjoy a perfect cappuccino, get in some good people-watching, and duck in from the rain. Yes, it's got a great communal table. But this time we preferred well-placed perches designed for two over a (perfectly welcoming) table for ten. There's something about seeing so many people comfortably standing and sipping that makes Monmouth feel abuzz beyond the caffeine. Open to the street on one side, making it feel a bit like a stage, this is a surprisingly cozy spot, thanks to heat lamps, great service, and lots of friendly chatter.

EVER NOTICE that people who live in places such as London, Seattle, and other cities where weather is tentative at best really know how to make the most of a sunny day?

47

SERPENTINE SOLAR SHUTTLE

HYDE PARK | The Boathouse, Serpentine Road | **SOLARSHUTTLE.ORG** | 020 7262 1330

We opted for a solar-boat ride across the Serpentine. It's a lovely, quiet, Earth-friendly ride (powered entirely by the sun) and provides a great vantage point for people-watching. Up front, there are three captain's wheels. One for the captain and two smaller ones for budding young seafarers. But before long, it was the other boats around us that caught our attention. This entry is dedicated to something we like to call Boaters Behaving Badly. Just because you've been given a small water vessel doesn't mean you know what to do with it. Instead of paying attention to where they were going, we saw most people who had rented paddleboats and rowboats chatting on cell phones, stranded or stuck on the ropes, stopping to have a cigarette, or our favorites: those who were just stopping to stand up and have a stretch.

THIS PLACE HAS BEEN AROUND long enough that the crowd is an odd mix of Scandinavian businessmen, models, middle-age couples, and rock stars.

SKETCH

MAYFAIR | 9 Conduit Street | **SKETCH.UK.COM** | 087 0777 4488

Sometimes places "try too hard" and sometimes they try so hard that they actually end up being delightful. Part art gallery, part restaurant, part bar and members' club, Sketch felt most like an evening at an urban amusement park, with every room taking you on a new ride. It's packed full of surprising novelties like a (bath)room filled with human-size eggs that looks more like an alien invasion than a W.C., and a circular bar that's bugged so you can eavesdrop on half of someone's conversation—and they on yours. Sometimes silly and decidedly over-the-top, what we found most pleasing at Sketch was observing others' moments of delight and discovery. It's hard not to enjoy yourself when the waiter instructs you to play with your food or a bathroom giggles when you close the door. Love it or hate it, Sketch will deliver some of the best experiential choreography you'll find on- or off-stage in London.

THEATRE

Theatre is everywhere in London. On a painstakingly presented dinner plate. In a lively monologue given by a black-cab driver. Floating above you at the bar at Hakkasan restaurant in Westminster. In patterns that play out floor to floor at Liberty of London [34]. Of course, let's not forget the experience of going to the theatre itself. The rich tradition and well-earned expertise on the London stage has inspired an entire city to create drama, comedy, interest, or intrigue at almost every turn. While you shouldn't miss a visit to the theatre while you're in London, we implore you to explore the idea that theatre—here more than most places—is everywhere.

WHAT'S CARROM? We don't know, but we like it. The Carrom Shop in Sunday Up Market has some of the best masala chai west of Mumbai.

SUNDAY UP MARKET

SHOREDITCH | Ely's Yard, The Old Truman Brewery, 91 Brick Lane | **SUNDAYUPMARKET.CO.UK** | 020 7770 6028

Equal parts heart and art for the anti-corporate crowd, Up Market is a downmarket response to New Spitalfields and a great place to see how temporary communities are formed. "There are always new artists coming and going. You don't see the same stuff in the same stalls week after week," said a woman selling woolly scarves and playful pillows. We came for the craft of it all, but we wound up really enjoying the sense of community. A transient tribe, coming together for something they believe in; stall keepers watching over each other's wares as if they were their own children. Community boards. Communal tables. Camaraderie. Carrom tables. Cupcakes. What more could you want?

Double hot
Dragon
Cocktail

Ye Olde Cheshire Cheese

REBUILT 1667

WITH HISTORY that includes famous authors, modern-day cultural icons, Carmelite monks, and tourists from the Midwest, how could you not be curious?

YE OLDE CHESHIRE CHEESE

CITY OF LONDON | 145 Fleet Street | 020 7353 6170

Yes, it's one of the oldest pubs in the City of London, dating back to 1667, and yes, Charles Dickens hung out here. It is also true that you may never find your way through the warren of rooms to every corridor, chamber, and anteroom. But if you get a chance, do explore some of the small, intimate spaces leading all the way down to the cellar, which, by the way, was once home to a thirteenth-century Carmelite monastery. While we were busy exploring, a waiter drew our attention to a large pile of dusty books discreetly set atop a bookshelf in the front dining room, each thoughtfully signed by hundreds of guests. "Would you like to see the one Madonna wrote?" he asked. Or how about the one penned by a survivor of the *Titanic*? Flip through and see how many people have enjoyed a pint or two, a hot meal, or the company of the likes of Mark Twain. Indeed, getting lost inside Ye Olde Cheshire Cheese can be quite a find.

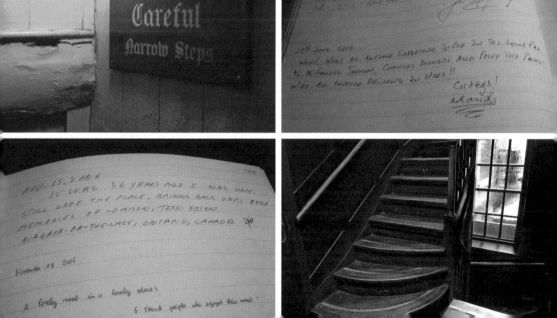

HOW THIS BOOK HAPPENED

Trying to find fifty really interesting experiences that will appeal to a diverse group of people requires talking to a lot of other people and walking a lot of streets. Here's a snapshot of how *Open Eyes* actually came together.

COMMUNITY CANVAS

To land on fifty experiences that our team could agree were book-worthy, we started with hundreds. And to get hundreds, we started the way many IDEO projects start: with an invitation to the worldwide IDEO community asking them to send us their most interesting submissions for each city. In true IDEO spirit, the floodgates opened and the e-mails came pouring in.

SORT & EDIT

To narrow down the potentials, we gathered an editorial board: Amy Leventhal (our writer and vegan chef), Sara Frisk (our communication designer and hipster mom), George Aye (our photographer and entrepreneur), Shane Parton (our project manager and rock singer), Fred Dust (our north star and experience junkie), and Allison Arieff (because she just seems so wise and worldly). Together we edited the submissions down to a manageable stack with all kinds of highly subjective criteria. The days were long and conversation intense, but we ended with somewhere in the vicinity of ninety submissions.

IN THE FIELD

Amy and Fred went out and experienced the locations firsthand, treating this research in much the same way we would approach other field work. Trying to be as open-minded as possible, we asked a lot of questions, explored beyond the list we came with, took copious notes, photographed like crazy so we could share back with the team, and talked about what we saw until our tonsils hurt. It sounds fun and it was, but those were also some of the most exhausting days we'd ever spent. By the end of the trip, we narrowed the list to sixty to seventy locations.

STORYTELLING

In small groups, with various team members dropping in, we edited the submissions and looked for themes and overlaps. We shared our stories and sussed out the reactions we received. Throughout this time, we chatted the ideas up with people inside and outside of IDEO to get a range of responses and finally landed on approximately fifty locations and ten themes.

FURTHER EXPLORATION

This time George and Shane went into the field to get inspired, photograph, and get permission to include each of the locations chosen. While getting to know some of the proprietors better, they uncovered new and interesting insights, which they then fed back to Amy as she started writing. New ideas were brought forth and others fell by the wayside. Once or twice when permission was declined, it was back to the huddle to fill in the gaps.

BUILDING THE BOOK

Along the way we mapped it, fact-checked it, edited it, second-guessed it, reviewed it, and tweaked it some more while Sara investigated countless ways to represent the books visually. After completing color and typeface studies, layout and sizing mock-ups, and sorting and organizational structures, hundreds (out of thousands) of photographs were selected and placed. Many late nights and toner cartridges later, something akin to "finished" began to emerge. The result is what you are holding in your hands. We hope you enjoy reading it as much as we enjoyed creating it.

[Photos from left to right] Sort & Edit at IDEO San Francisco, Fred literally in the field, Amy at the Kandy Team Room, George in London, Shane at Labour and Wait, Sara at IDEO Chicago

ACKNOWLEDGMENTS

Everyone we talked with during the making of this book thought
we were the luckiest people on Earth to get an opportunity to do
something like this. We assured each one of them that it was grueling,
exhausting, and at times overwhelming. (No one bought our story,
but it was 100 percent true!) However, now that the deadlines have
passed, our feet have stopped aching, and our frequent flyer miles
have added up, we really must admit that everyone was right.
We feel so lucky to have been a part of the Eyes Open series.

EYES OPEN LONDON TEAM

George Aye
Fred Dust
Sara Frisk
Amy Leventhal
Shane Parton

BUT WE CERTAINLY COULDN'T
HAVE DONE IT ALL WITHOUT A
LITTLE HELP FROM OUR FRIENDS...

HELPING HANDS

Very special thanks to Alan Rapp at Chronicle Books and the many kind folks who gave us permission to include their establishments in this book.

A great big "we owe you one" to some friends and fellow IDEOers who lent their skills along the way: Allison Arieff, Paul Bennett, Miguel Cabra, Kate Canales, Sally Clark, Paul Edmunds, Joseph Graceffa, Ian Groulx, Alexa Hagerty, Kathleen Hughes, Andrea Koerselman, Evan Krasner, Whitney Mortimer, Brenda Natoli, Flora Saldivar, Scott Sauer, Louise Wainwright, Richard Weaver, and Marc Woollard.

TESTIMONIALS

If not for the following people, we would never have found a good many of the great locations featured in this book: Ingrid Baron, Tim Brown, Miguel Cabra, Valeria Cardoso, Clive Cheesman, Alexa Hagerty, Gitte Jonsdatter, Devorah Klein, Georgie Mack, Naslee Parker, Will Rosenzweig, Fran Samalionis, Neil Stevenson, Jamie Styles, Pontus Walgren, and Bryan Walker.

PHOTOGRAPHY

Thanks to the following London locations for graciously providing us with additional photography:

[2] Dinosaur Hall: photos used with permission from the Natural History Museum, London

[5] Miller's Academy: bottom left portrait courtesy of Miller's Academy, photographed by Sasha Gusov

[21] The Wolseley: all photos courtesy of and © The Wolseley

[27] Daylesford Organic: exterior and interior photos courtesy of Daylesford Organic at Clifton Nurseries London

[37] Paul Smith: photos of clothing courtesy of Paul Smith

[42] Electric Cinema: bottom left photo courtesy of Electric Cinema

SITE INDEX

WHAT DO YOU WANT TO SEE?

try the

_____

try the

_____

try the

_____

go here with

_____

go here with

_____

go here with

_____

don't miss

_____

don't miss

_____

don't miss

_____

best between

_____ am/pm

best between

_____ am/pm

best between

_____ am/pm

bring my

_____

bring my

_____

bring my

_____

yum

_____

yum

_____

yum

_____